The Lady of the Water

The Story of SS *KOOPA*, 1911-1953

Colin Jones and David Jones

Published by:
Boolarong Press
655 Toohey Road
Salisbury Qld 4107
Australia
www.boolarongpress.com.au

National Library of Australia Cataloguing-in-Publication entry:
Creator: Jones, Colin, 1941- author.

Title:	The lady of the water : the story of SS Koopa, 1911-1953 / Colin Jones and David Jones.
ISBN:	9781925236224 (paperback)
Subjects:	SS Koopa (Ship)--History. Steamboats--Queensland--Moreton Bay--History. Boats and boating--Queensland--Moreton Bay. Moreton Bay (Qld.)--History.
Other Creators/Contributors:	
	Jones, David (David Embry), 1945- author.
Dewey Number:	387.2044

Cover Design by Boolarong Press.

Cover Picture: *Koopa*, the lady of the water, between the wars (Queensland Maritime Museum collection)

Printed and bound by Watson Ferguson & Company, Salisbury, Brisbane, Australia.

The Lady of the Water

The Story of SS *KOOPA*, 1911-1953

Colin Jones and David Jones

Koopa steams under the Story Bridge on 13 December 1952.
(photo by Mervyn Jones, C & D Jones collection ©)

Contents

Acknowledgements

We acknowledge with thanks all who have provided photos for inclusion in this book. In particular we express our gratitude to the State Library of Queensland, the Queensland Maritime Museum, Moreton Bay Region Libraries and the Australian War Memorial for photos and information made available and used.

The National Library of Australia's 'trove' digital database of Australian newspapers has been an invaluable resource, helping fill out or confirm matters of detail throughout *Koopa*'s working life. 'Trove' is a vital tool for anyone researching matters of Australian or family history and we salute the National Library's efforts in making this available for the benefit of all.

Our sincere thanks go to David Gibson, eminent historian of all things Brisbane, and to Ian Jempson, historian and CEO of the Queensland Maritime Museum, for their endorsements to this book. They are much appreciated.

Most of all we pay a deep and sincere tribute to our parents, Mervyn and Heather Jones. They introduced us to the *Koopa* and Moreton Bay at an early age, and gave us a warm affection for Redcliffe through a series of family holidays there in the 1950s.

Colin Jones, David Jones
March 2015

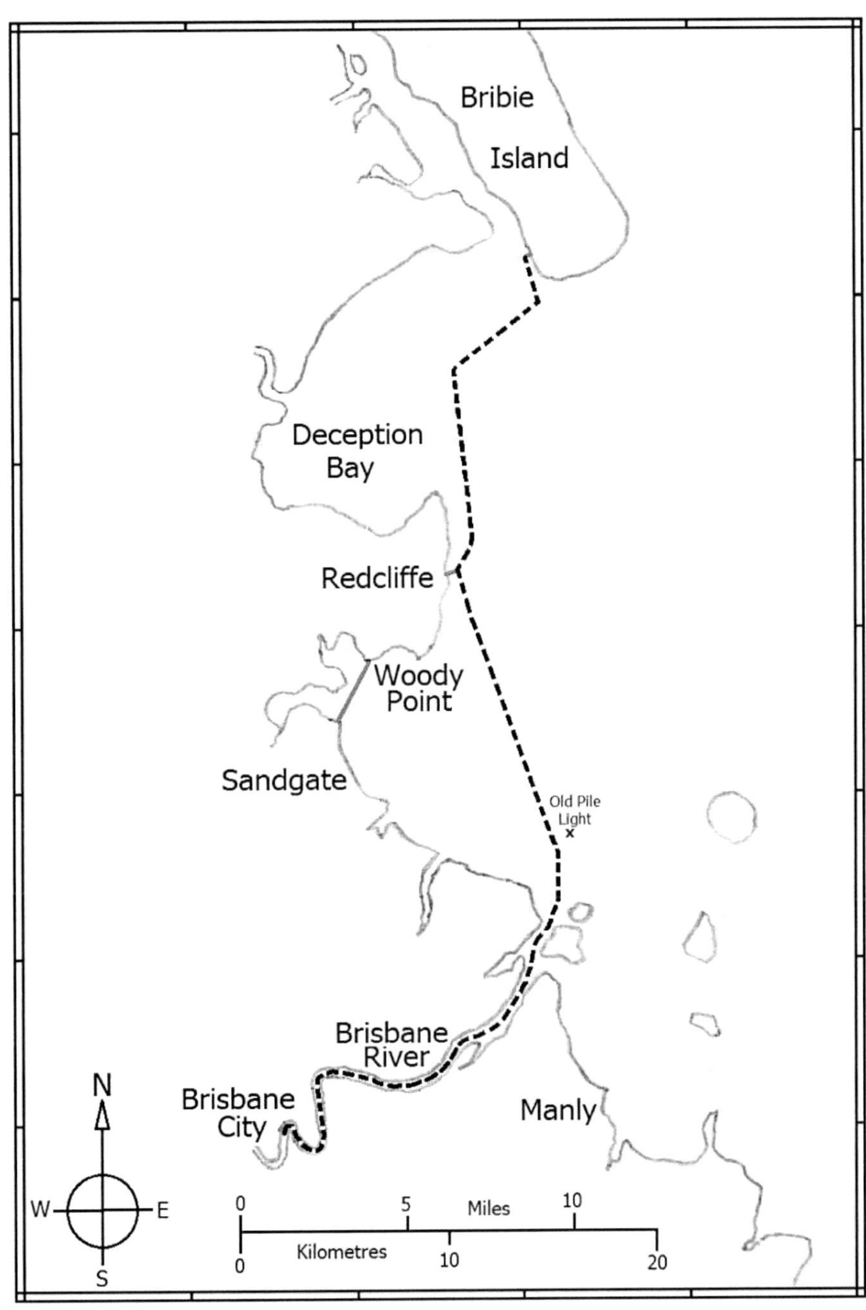

Koopa's customary route across Moreton Bay

The Lady of the Water

Brisbane is a city built on a river. Broad and brown as it twists through the city, it belies its destination in the blue waters of Moreton Bay, not so very far away. To the Brisbane person the Bay has a magic. The old aborigine knew it as he and the dolphin hunted together for the basking flathead, and generations of later piscatorials in their boats have searched the Bay for their finny quarry, especially the superb schnapper. The schnapper was regarded as the best fish in Australian waters, a good big fish, worth the catching. There were often steamer charters to go to the best spots beyond Cape Moreton. If you didn't have any luck and had to buy your fish at the market on the way home, you were said to use 'silver bait'. Men who went out on the steamer to fish considered themselves a cut above those who fished from the beach, and called them the 'Band of Hope'. There were also the yachtsmen, enjoying themselves so much that they might pretend to be weatherbound somewhere in the Bay on Monday morning to account for their absence from work. The modern generation of motor boat enthusiasts have no such excuse. Moreton Bay evolved boats of a particular design, typically a 23 foot centreboard gaff cutter, strong and easy to sail, as all such boats should be. Some would race, and some would just enjoy the water. But perhaps many people would say the Bay is best seen from the deck of a smart steamer, on the sea road to Redcliffe or to the long sandy islands floating on the eastern horizon. The Rainbow Channel, though named after a ship, always promises something special about the water, deep blue between the sands. There was the sea breeze on the upper deck under the awnings, and in the evening one could watch the sub-tropical night arising out of the land, the wash of the other excursion steamers coming in together, and the lights of the city of Brisbane, on its seven hills.

It always amazes the Brisbane person that Matthew Flinders missed the River completely. How could you miss something so big? Yet it was different in his time, and it was not until the early 20th century that the long training walls were built, and dredging gave access up to Kangaroo Point by a 24 foot channel, with 26 feet to

New Farm. The Dalgety Wharf at New Farm dates from 1907 and the arrival of the Blue Funnel *Nestor* there in 1913 was a milestone for the size of ships. At the mouth of the River, the new bar cutting was completed in 1912, and the pile lighthouse was moved to cover it, though the spindly frame of old piles was left in place. The port was full of shipping, and the developments that followed. The first reinforced concrete wharf in Queensland was built at Hamilton in 1922, to serve the new cool stores.

To get to the beach at Southport or Tweed Heads you went by train, but for Redcliffe, it was a trip on the sea. Usually the traveller to what was then, for lack of adequate land routes, virtually an island, would take the train to Shorncliffe and walk over the hill to the jetty where he would find the 'fine saloon motor launch *Olivine*', which, from 1909 to 1928 ran five times per day across the water to Woody Point jetty, the nearest point of the Redcliffe peninsula. On some trips she would continue to Redcliffe jetty, and sometimes it could be a bit rough. There was no Redcliffe railway. Food and other supplies went by ship. On four days per week a ferry steamer would leave Birkbeck's Wharf in Brisbane for Queensport, Lytton, Woody Point and Redcliffe. Some trips extended to Scarborough and Bribie Island. From 1884 to 1900 this service was run by the 90 foot steamer *Garnet*. In view of the increased popularity of Redcliffe, in 1891 she was extensively rebuilt for an improved service with a speed of 10 knots. She could reach Woody Point in two hours and eight minutes. But in 1900 she was replaced by a larger vessel, the *Emerald*. She was a wooden vessel of 189 tons, 124 feet long and powered by compound engines for a speed of 11 knots. She was licensed for 800 passengers in the River and 487 in the Bay. The Tuesday and Thursday 9.30am runs from Kennedy's Wharf at Petrie Bight were only lightly patronised by commercial travellers, local people visiting the city, holidaying families and the like, but on Saturday and Sunday she would be crowded with excursionists on as many as three trips a day. Captain Bengt Fridolf (Barney) Bengston, who had supervised her construction in Sydney, transferred from the *Garnet* to be her master.

The launch *Olivine*, which connected Sandgate with Woody Point from 1909 to 1928. (George Mewes photo, Moreton Bay Region Libraries image. no.000055)

The steamer *Emerald*, introduced on the Redcliffe run in 1900. (John Oxley Library, State Library of Queensland neg.152226)

She was advertised as having a spacious saloon, a ladies' room, dinners, oysters, refreshments and 'Afternoon Tea of the Best'. A plate of oysters with bread and butter could be had for 1/-. Fares were Adult 1/6, Return 2/6, Children 6d each way. Fares on the *Olivine* were Single 1/-, Return 1/6, Children 6d each way. Both vessels were owned by the Humpybong Steamship Company. Humpybong – every school child knew that the name was an aboriginal word for Dead Houses, applied to the Redcliffe area after the departure in 1825 of the convict settlers to the more attractive site of Brisbane.

Yacht regattas, especially at Queen's Birthday in May and Prince of Wales' Birthday in November, would be sure to attract a whole flotilla of steamers, with the passengers crowded to the rail to see the flying sails. The *Emerald* might be the flagship for the races. Competition in the excursion field was provided by the Brisbane Tug Company Ltd, whose three tugs, *Boko*, *Greyhound* and *Beaver* were all equipped to take passengers on holidays and weekends when not required for towage. Unlike modern tugs, they had extended upper deck areas for passengers, as excursion work was a major part of their trade. The *Boko* was a paddler, and you might well be aboard her to watch a yacht race, for an up-river excursion, or as a member of the militia going into camp. The jetty at Woody Point was built 700 feet long, with a big dog-leg out into a sufficient depth of water for the *Boko* to use. A favourite trip was to the southern tip of Moreton Island at South Passage for surf bathing, fish and oyster meals, and the convivial glass at the ship's bar.

The company considered that another spot worthy of development would be Bribie Island, and they commenced fishing excursions there with the *Greyhound*, passengers being ferried ashore at Bongaree in boats. After the *Emerald* had carried some 3,000 people to Redcliffe over the Christmas week of 1905, it was plain that a new steamer was needed for the Bay excursion trade. After raising new capital and re-formatting the tug company as the Brisbane Tug and Steamship Company Ltd in February 1911, a steamer was ordered from Ramage & Ferguson Ltd of Leith, Scotland, especially suited to Moreton Bay conditions.

Crowded with sightseers, the *Beaver*'s career as tug and excursion vessel covered almost sixty years. (Queensland Maritime Museum collection)

Crowds on Redcliffe jetty greet the arrival of the *Emerald* in 1909. (Murray Photos, John Oxley Library, State Library of Queensland image no.TR1867-0001-0008)

Her draught was to be limited so that she could use the Woody Point jetty, which had a depth of water of only eight feet at low tide. Her name was *Koopa,* the delightfully onomatopoeic aboriginal word for a flying fish – you hear the sound of it as it hits the water.

Particulars of the new ship were:

Steel hull, twin screw steamship;
Tonnage: 679 displacement, 416 gross, 170 net;
Length: 202.2' overall, 192.6' bp; Beam 28.1';
Depth: 9.27' moulded and 16'6" to the promenade deck;
Draught: 6'6" aft; Freeboard 2'6";
Length of promenade deck 140';
Four watertight steel bulkheads;
Licensed to carry 1,153 passengers on the Bay and 2,000 on the River [1];
Maximum speed on trials 15.5 knots while developing 1,450 ihp, with a best run at 16.5 knots and continuous sea speed of 14 knots;
Two triple expansion engines, cylinders 13", 21" & 34", and 18" stroke; two single ended multi-tube Scotch boilers @ 180 psi, with Howden's forced draft; Bunkers 80 tons coal;
12 Boyle's patent ventilators.

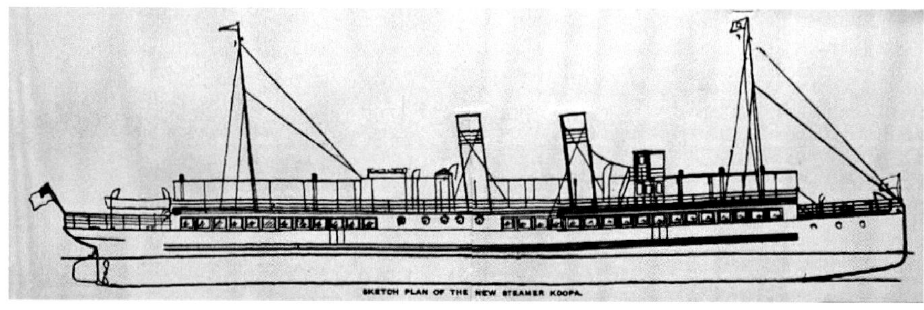

Sketch plan of the new steamer *Koopa* published in Brisbane's press before her arrival. (*The Brisbane Courier*, 17 October 1911)

[1] Until 1914, two children counted for one adult.

Other features were a dining saloon and a bar the full width of the ship on the main deck forward, and another dining saloon and pantry aft, with two-speed electric fans in both, and 'railway carriage' sash windows that could be opened as required. The galley amidships could serve 50 people at a time and there would always be boiling water for tea. For the children, a confectionery stall was at the after end of the main deck. On the lower deck were two more saloons, separated by the engine and boiler rooms. The captain's cabin and ticket office were on the promenade deck, officers' accommodation below and crew's quarters in the forecastle.

Ramage & Ferguson specialised in tugs and small merchant ships. In the 1880s they had built the *Otter* and *Beaver*, both well thought of, as well as the steam yacht *Merrie England*, bought for the New Guinea administration. They had built some pretty craft. The *Koopa* was to be something special. Her cost was £20,000.

The *Koopa* was launched on 15 September 1911 and after trials on 14 October, completed and left Leith under the command of Captain Robert Douglas Taylor six days later. In the English Channel she met heavy weather and was forced to shelter off Margate and later in Portsmouth. She made most of her passage on one boiler only, which gave her a speed of 11 knots, but in the Bay of Biscay both boilers were fired and on three successive days she steamed 332, 328 and 290 miles, an average of up to 14 knots. Calls for coal and water were made at Gibraltar, Port Said, Perim (southern entrance to the Red Sea), Colombo, Batavia, Thursday Island, Cooktown and Townsville. Captain J. Peebles was the pilot south from Thursday Island, from where she departed on 18 December and Captain Taylor reported that the ship had suffered no damage whatsoever on the trip out, and had shown 'a fine turn of speed'. On his arrival in Brisbane he became manager and secretary of the tug company until his death in 1943.

Dressed in flags, *Koopa* draws a large crowd for her first excursion on Christmas Day, 1911. (John Oxley Library, State Library of Queensland neg.158494)

Koopa's inaugural crew with her long-serving master, Captain Jack Johnston, seated in the centre. (John Oxley Library, State Library of Queensland neg.37321)

To work her, the *Koopa* carried a captain, mate, three seamen, three firemen, two engineers, a deck boy and six catering staff. The aft dining saloon could seat 100 people.

Meanwhile in Brisbane the *Koopa's* itinerary was being announced for the Christmas holiday period before she had even made port. Her first cruise was to be to Redcliffe on the afternoon of Christmas Day, leaving Brisbane at 2.30pm and Redcliffe at 5pm. In anticipation, the Redcliffe Shire Council had repairs done to the jetty, where one of the piles had recently broken. On Christmas Eve of 1911 the *Koopa* entered the Brisbane River for the first time, and she was met off Hamilton by company and other officials in the *Greyhound*, and given a clean bill of health. Crowds were waiting for her on the tug company's wharf by the Customs House as she rounded Kangaroo Point, flags gaily flying from both masts, but she steamed straight past to the South Brisbane railway wharf to coal about 5pm. Her new master was to be Captain John Scott (Jack) Johnston, who had been master of the *Emerald* from 1909 after the death of Captain Bengston. Prior to that, he was master of W'm Collin & Sons' *Lady Musgrave* trading to the Richmond River. He was a man who knew every last aspect of Moreton Bay. With the advent of the *Doomba* in 1923 he transferred to her, but when she was laid up in 1928 he returned to the *Koopa.* Engineer J. G. Campbell also served in both ships. Under Captain Johnston's care the *Koopa* made smart passages across the Bay year after year, 'the greyhound of the River'. Even with the south-easter smashing the waves against Redcliffe jetty to blow spray in the faces of people waiting, he would bring his ship alongside as safely as if it were flat calm. In the River itself, she was not bound by a rule to travel at no more than six knots, as her draught was less than seven feet, but her wash would often leave small boats bobbing, especially if they were fishing too close to the channel. The *Koopa* was a big beautiful vessel, 'one of the finest and handsomest coastal craft in Queensland', and proved instantly very popular. According to the advertisements, the Promenade, Main Deck and Saloons were brilliantly lighted throughout with electric light by no fewer than 159 lamps in all. It was also stated 'This steamer is very fast. Excursionists are specially reminded that the *Koopa* will have no difficulty keeping to the timetable'. Prices were the same as those on the *Emerald,* and the two ships would leave within minutes of each other, black smoke pouring from their funnels; but it would soon become obvious which was the better ship as they reached the broad waters of Moreton Bay. The *Koopa* just walked away from the older ship.

The constricted area around the River wharves was the cause of an accident on 12 March 1912 when the *Oswestry Grange* was endeavouring to berth upstream, and was forced into a collision with the *Koopa*, lying at her usual place. There was considerable damage to the awning but Captain Johnston saved the port lifeboat by lowering it off its davits onto the deck. In July she was hauled out on Peter's Slip at Kangaroo Point to have four-bladed bronze screws fitted to replace the original three-bladed ones. These had come out from Scotland with her, along with a spare tail shaft, and were expected to increase her speed and eliminate vibration. At the same time her after saloon was enlarged and permanent wooden sun awnings were fitted in place of the original canvas.

Koopa on Peter's Slip with the cross-river vehicular ferry *Brisbane*. (Queensland Maritime Museum collection)

In her early years the *Koopa* was used for excursions: Redcliffe and Bribie, Ocean Beach at South Passage, (lunch aboard provided by Barney Phillips) and day and night cruises to the Pile Light or afternoon trips around Mud Island or to Tangalooma. The *Beaver* might take the overflow crowd. Unfortunately, the constantly shifting sand proved too much of a handicap for the jetty to be maintained on the southern end of Moreton Island for the Ocean Beach surfing trips, which were abandoned. From 16 December 1912 a special 6.50am departure from Redcliffe was introduced every Monday, arriving in Brisbane by 8.45am in time for work. At New Year 1913 the *Koopa* ran to Redcliffe at 9.30am, the *Beaver* to Bribie and the *Boko* to South Passage. During the Christmas holidays in 1913 the *Koopa* ran to Redcliffe and Bribie twice a day, the *Emerald* from her new berth a bit further downstream, to Woody Point in the evening, and the *Beaver* to Redcliffe on a late night voyage. On occasion, the *Emerald* would call at Mowbray Park. However in May 1914 the *Emerald* was sold to the Commonwealth Government and sent to Western Australia to help build the new naval base, and the *Koopa* inherited the four days per week Redcliffe ferry service. Passengers from, Norman Park and Mowbray Park could come up to join the ship in the motor launch *Beryl*, and from Hamilton, she would stop to pick up passengers from boats if required.

Compared with the long sleek lines of the *Koopa*, the *Emerald* had appeared stubby, slow and old-fashioned. The *Koopa* was beautiful in her grey and white paint and her long shady awnings, with the red band of the tug company on her funnels. People at the rustic bayside resort of Beachmere could set their watches by the *Koopa* passing offshore at midday. Redcliffe, compared with the city, was a rather sandy, unpainted place where you took off your collar and tie, even though it had suburbs with English seaside names such as Margate and Scarborough. You could relax at Redcliffe. But Bribie was like a wilderness, and full of wildflowers in the spring. For Bribie there was no option. Everything there had to come by ship, even the building materials for houses. Cargo aboard the *Koopa* would be up to 40 tons of mixed items, from cement and gravel to groceries and milk. Brisbane to Bribie was a round trip of 76 miles.

Redcliffe jetty with SS *Emerald* alongside from a postcard. (Edco Series postcard No.1496 sent on 22 April 1911, C & D Jones collection)

There had been an urgent need for a jetty at Bribie, and the tug company built a 200 foot structure with a depth of water alongside of 20 feet at low tide. It was completed in May 1912 and on 4 June the company ran a special shareholders' excursion, flags flying, with lunch served on the upper deck. The many guests included the mayors of both Brisbane and South Brisbane.

Such were the crowds that the walkways to the Bribie jetty had to be secured by gates, under the supervision of Bill Freeman, whose house was nearby. The tug company had to bring the drinking water, and it built a boarding house, lunch rooms, and twelve holiday huts, soon called the Twelve Apostles, which stood near the jetty. Tea tree poles were available for tents. Ash from the ship's furnaces went to help make a more solid road across the sand. As there was no pub on the island, anyone wanting a couple of quiet ales would have to visit the *Koopa's* bar while she was tied up. In the springtime, local people brought great bunches of flowering boronia to sell to the passengers. The tug company sponsored the Bribie Shield surf lifesaving competition from 1927.

Another curiosity of the 1930s was the Novelty Gardens, where hedges were sculpted into the shape of birds and animals.

Koopa at the newly completed jetty on Bribie Island during an excursion for company shareholders on 4 June 1912. (John Oxley Library, State Library of Queensland neg.24336)

Although the route to Redcliffe jetty was straight across from the turn at the Old Pile Light, the voyage from there to Bribie had several changes of course, to avoid rocks off Redcliffe, and the sandbars of the Western Banks off Bribie.

This is what it was like.

Early on Saturday morning the family is away into town on the tram to go for a trip on the *Koopa*. There are crowds already at Circular Quay, so the children race aboard while father is presenting the tickets at the gangway, to claim suitable seats by the rail, a position consolidated by a blanket and the picnic baskets.

Grandma will be content to sit there and take the breeze. Dogs are tied up so as not to get under people's feet. A big pile of boxes and crates for the Bribie Island shopkeepers is under a tarpaulin between the funnels. The slow leak of water across the deck shows where the ice is packed in sawdust and hessian bags.

Stylishly dressed holiday-makers flock to board the *Koopa* and *Beaver* at their Brisbane terminal during the *Koopa*'s first month of service. (*The Queenslander*, 13 January 1912)

Some young people are already out on the bow where they will in due course be suffering the rigours of sunburn. This is a world of ships, of scrubbed timber and polished brass, and the smell of steam. There is a long deck, and stairways with polished rails, so the children run around excitedly. Across the way are the black and white funnels of the Howard Smith steamers *Cooma* and *Koonawarra*. At another wharf upstream, beyond the handsome facade of the Customs House, the black funnel with two white bands belongs to the AUSN *Wodonga*, bound for Gladstone,

Mackay, Bowen and Townsville. 9.30am; a blast on the whistle as the gangways are removed and the moorings cast off; the screws churn vigorously at the muddy river water and the ship is away. The riverbank at Kangaroo Point is full of slipways, sheds and cranes, but further along there are the big houses by the waterside with their wide verandahs shaded by fig and mango trees; the little cross-river motor ferry pitching wildly as it crosses our wake; yachts at moorings; big freighters, maybe an overseas liner. The *Changsha* will be sailing for Zamboanga, Manila, China and Japan, while the *Yawata Maru* has scheduled Townsville, Thursday Island, Manila, Hong Kong and Japan. *Tydeus*, a Blue Funnel liner – does that mean rain? Tugboats too, maybe the new powerful twin funnelled *Coringa*.

Crowds disembark from the *Koopa* at Redcliffe jetty in 1925 at the height of her popularity. (Moreton Bay Region Libraries image. no.000117)

Father notes that the bar is open after Hamilton, though he does not want to appear too eager in front of the family. The dredges and barges are moored in the River. Perhaps there will be signs of an accident, like the *Dolphin*, sunk by the *Bombala* near Lytton. As the River opens into the Bay, father has stoked up his pipe and is deeply engrossed in the pages of the *Courier*, while mother has thought it about time for a nice cup of tea in the saloon. There is Fort Lytton with its six-inch guns, there is the Luggage Point sewage outlet with the mangroves, and the gulls circling. Someone is bound to tell the joke about the person who fell in about here – he couldn't swim but he went through the motions. And, as the water opens out, there are the islands of the Bay; St Helena with its gaol, Moreton with its great sandhills, highest in the world. Look over the side, maybe you will see hordes of jellyfish. The white sails are yachts off Sandgate. Once the spindly form of the Old Pile Light is left behind the *Koopa* uses the old channel, not the Bar Cutting. It is often called the Koopa Channel. Now one can start to make out the details of the dark red cliffs that gave Redcliffe its name. There is Victoria House at Woody Point, the 'wedding cake house', with its two levels of verandahs and lookout tower on top of the roof. Soon the big buildings are clear - the Hotel Redcliffe or the Seabrae boarding house among the trees. It is almost 11.30am as we come in to Redcliffe; people are swimming, or sitting on the beach; the soft sand and the red rocks; Redcliffe.

Koopa backs away from Redcliffe jetty, homeward bound with a full load of passengers. (Jean Bassett collection, Moreton Bay Region Libraries image. no.001019)

Water surges from the screws as the ship is stopped to come alongside, and the crew are ready to throw the mooring ropes. The jetty is lined with people, and some much-envied children are being ushered away from running up and down with the baggage trolley. Most people disembark here and some come aboard for the hour's run across to Bribie Island. The channel of the Pumicestone Passage is deep by the island, with a strong tidal current, and the *Koopa* lies quite close inshore against the jetty. All the Bribie people are out, as the arrival of the ship is the big event of the day. There is a heavy trolley on the jetty to carry the boxes and parcels. A boy is towed down the gangway by a large panting dog. A couple of local boats have come by selling crayfish and fruit. Mother assesses them with a keen eye.

Koopa and local crayfish sellers' boats rest beside Bribie Island jetty during the 1920s (St Paul's School website www.stpauls.qld.edu.au/paulipedia)

Time for lunch under a tree, for sandwiches, cakes and cordial, a swim, and back aboard ready to leave at 3pm. The children are pink and covered in sand and some have pieces of pumice in their hands – it will be good for the bathroom later. Passengers have already been warned by the ship's whistle, well ahead of time, as there is no other way home if you are lost in the tea tree. Captain Johnston is standing on the bridge wing watching closely the way the ship is handled. In the distance are the Glasshouse Mountains, named by Captain Cook.

Back at Redcliffe jetty the crowds of holiday-makers troop aboard, red noses poking out under straw hats. Many of the children have red dirt on clothes that were once clean. And so we set out for home. The south-easter will have built up the swells, and the ship heaves as it turns across the bar into the River. The young people out on the bow are now wet from spray as well as sunburnt, and come to look for somewhere more sheltered. Someone is bound to lose a hat. A few less hardy souls look to the leeward rail. At the mouth of the river the *Beaver* falls in astern for the passage upstream. The *Otter* is in sight from her regular run to Dunwich. At 6pm the *Koopa* has tied up again at her berth just by the Customs House. For the crew of the *Koopa* after passing Hamilton is the time to relax a bit. The head of steam she has here will take her all the way to the city.

The *Koopa* departing Redcliffe for Bribie Island in 1935.
(Queensland Maritime Museum collection.)

A sentimental Melbourne visitor encapsulated the whole ethos of carefree holiday Redcliffe in 1916, with his description of the bathing and the sundry eccentric ways of dressing for the beach. He also noted the superior attitude of 'the week-ender and holiday-maker' to the 'day tripper'. The boarding houses displayed 'decorative designs of drying towels, bathing gowns and white boots'. On the beach people would be arguing politics or reading 'the romances of the American yellow back fiction writers', swimming, paddling, or just looking into one another's eyes. So evening came. 'The light of the steamer in the distance causes a stir in the crowd who are waiting to welcome loved ones released from the bounds of business.' And so back on the ship there were 'the creakings of the hawsers and the shouts of the sailors, the pier and its dimly outlined figures' fading away. The return on the *Koopa* saw the pleasure 'greatly magnified ... when, after a tropical day, the beautiful night breezes come stealing along the river, playing with the spear shaped reflected lights on the river and kissing the wearied and hot brow of the tripper.'

Koopa surges past the Apollo ferry on Hamilton Reach between the wars. (photo by Heather Jones, C & D Jones collection)

The Great War had come close with the arrival in Brisbane in October 1914 of the steamer *Southport*, which had escaped from the Caroline Islands after her engines were crippled by the crew of the German gunboat *Geier*. As the *Koopa* passed where she was berthed, Abe Barrington's band struck up 'Rule Britannia' and other patriotic tunes.

Later, servicemen returning from the war in France were glad to see the ship. Not only had the war been long, hard and brutal, but the influenza pandemic sweeping the world demanded a strict quarantine response to prevent it spreading to Australia. On 14 February 1919 the *Koopa* took 1,000 men from the *Nestor* up from the quarantine station at Lytton to Kennedy's Wharf. The ship had arrived three days earlier and was declared clean of infections. On 26 February the express steamer *Loongana* unloaded 346 soldiers and 23 British wives at Lytton to be brought up to the city by the *Koopa* three days later and welcomed with great joy. On 19 and 21 May, soldiers from the *Port Denison* and *Khyber* were transferred up the River by the *Beaver*, and the next day the *Koopa* met the *Dongala* near the Pile Light to take 542 men up to Kangaroo Point, where they were welcomed by family and friends in misty rain. On 24 March, 192 men and three nurses came from the *Delta*, to the hooting of ships' whistles as the *Koopa* came upstream. They had been quarantined in isolation there for a week.

There were trips to view special ships also. On 20 March the *Koopa* took people to see the White Star Line's 'giant' *Ceramic*, at 18,500 tons the largest ship in Australian waters, anchored off the Pile Light. 250 troops who had arrived on board were released from quarantine at Lytton on 26 March and brought up to the Kangaroo Point Hospital jetty by the *Koopa*. On 12 July it was an occasion to see HMAS *Platypus* and the five J class submarines that had just joined the navy, anchored off the Pile Light.

There was then a post-war boom, typified on St Andrew's Day 1921, when the Redcliffe jetty was host to four vessels, the *Koopa* and *Beaver* with school trips, the *Otter* with picnickers and the *Noosa* with cargo.

The imposing entrance to Redcliffe jetty in 1935. (John Oxley Library, State Library of Queensland image. 6798-0001-0002)

Following a survey in 1919, a new and longer jetty was completed at Redcliffe in January 1922, close to the old structure, which was then demolished. Construction at the rocky point to the south was considered inappropriate. It was built on concrete piers, 900 feet long, had a shelter shed at the half way mark, and gates to hold back the crowds while the steamer berthed. Entry to the jetty cost a penny. There was also a new sea wall and promenade. Another new jetty was built at Woody Point at the same time, to reach deeper water. For their opening celebrations on 4 March, the Governor, Sir Matthew Nathan, boarded the *Koopa* at 10am and arrived at Redcliffe at midday. Then after the appropriate official celebrations, he boarded the *Koopa* again at 1.45pm to sail to Woody Point, where he opened the Memorial School of Arts. Finally the ship sailed back to Brisbane with him at 4pm.

Labour relations could often be fraught. When seamen returned to the liner *Rimutaka* on 1 November 1925 police had to intervene violently to separate them from other seamen who remained on strike. The crew of the *Beaver* then refused to man her and the AUSN's *Fearless* was brought in to help the vessel out. Subsequent events continued to fester. On 19 December 1925 the tug company's employees went on strike demanding a 44-hour week, as provided by the State, but not the Federal Award. This was followed by the *Koopa*, *Doomba*, *Beaver* and *Greyhound* being declared 'black' by the Queensland Branch of the Federated Seamen's Union. A volunteer crew kept the *Koopa* running on a daily basis, much to the relief of those who were taking her for their Christmas holidays at Redcliffe, and who had arrived at the wharf in hope. Even when the dispute seemed close to resolution, men at the South Brisbane coal wharf refused to load the *Koopa* on 8 January and she returned to lie alongside a coal barge by Kangaroo Point. The volunteer crew arrived to help coal, to be greeted with scuffles and thrown bottles and rocks by the strikers. Even Captain Johnston's car, when he arrived, had bottles thrown at it. The arrival of the Water Police separated the groups and the *Koopa* was able to sail, though all the other company ships sat idle. The whole matter was settled before it could extend to the railways, on 9 January 1926.

The *Koopa* was often employed as flagship for races by the Royal Queensland Yacht Club, the men in white linen and the women in silk frocks and bright accessories. On 14 February 1923 the Albert Cup interstate race for 21 foot restricted class yachts was sailed on a 12 mile triangular course on Moreton Bay from the Pile Light. The Governor General, Lord Forster, entered his yacht *Corella*, but it was beaten by a local boat, *Miss Brisbane*. Sir Matthew Nathan himself donated a cup for an event in December 1924, on another triangular course from the Pile Light. Only when the skiff championships were moved to Waterloo Bay because of a flood flow in 1927 was she replaced by the launch *Radio*. On 11 January 1930 Alf Whereats's new skiff *Ajax V* triumphantly beat all opposition, and he was awarded the blue ribbon on the deck of the *Koopa* by Mrs N. Wright.

Koopa lists heavily to allow spectators a better view of the King's Cup rowing regatta on 13 May 1939. (www.couriermail.com.au 'our river, our city' gallery)

The world of boating was changing, as shown by the collision between the *Koopa* and the fast motor launch *Redwing* near the Hamilton retaining wall in June 1924. That August as part of the Brisbane Centenary celebrations, the new local wonder boat *Century Tire* showed her paces by easily beating the previous record holder *Meteor* in a race up the River. The *Doomba* was flagship for the occasion. A really big event saw the Griffith Cup hydroplane championships held in Brisbane for the first time on 21 February 1925. The *Century Tire* again showed off her paces as she roared up the measured mile from Hamilton Cool Stores to Breakfast Creek at 70 miles an hour. The *Doomba* was flagship instead of the *Koopa*, in view of her larger capacity. She had the Governor on board, while the *Koopa* and *Luana* and many small craft were all crowded with some of the 6,000 spectators. As in 1924, there was a race against an aeroplane, in this case Lieutenant Miller's Curtis seaplane, which was an easy winner. The *Koopa* and *Radio* both carried people to see the Commodore's Cup races in 1929. With the *Otter* as flagship, the *Koopa* was crowded with sightseers for the King's Cup rowing regatta at Hamilton in May 1933. A big load would make the ship heel right over as they crowded to one side. The Albert Cup was again held on the River on 4 February 1939, when the Governor, Sir Leslie Wilson was on board; and the *Koopa* presided over many more. When the King's Cup races were held in the Hamilton Reach on 5 May 1951 the *Koopa*, along with Hayles' *Majestic*, took sightseers, while the police closed all of the riverside roads.

At Redcliffe, the Pier Theatre was built opposite the end of the jetty, in the growing shopping centre of Redcliffe Parade, in 1920. It seated 1,290 people, a wonder in a town which did not have a public electricity supply until 1928. The bright lights of the *Koopa*, too, would be a wonder in the dark town when she called at the jetty at night, as she did frequently on regular runs and special excursions. In August 1922, while the *Koopa* was on the slip and the *Beaver* had suffered an accident, the tug company hired the government steamer *Otter* for the Bay service.

Koopa's running mate *Doomba* trails a characteristic plume of smoke in the 1920s. (Whitehead collection, World Ship Society, Victoria)

By 1923, such was the popularity of the excursion service, often requiring the services of two steamers, that the *Koopa* was joined by a big sister, the *Doomba.* The new ship had been built as the *Wexford,* a minesweeping sloop for the British navy, but she was too late for the war and had been converted for the excursion trade.

After arrival in Brisbane on 4 August 1923 she was given a permanent awning. At 750 tons she was almost twice the size of the *Koopa.* She was 231 feet long and was faster also, with a speed of up to 19 knots when pressed, which often surprised the big overseas vessels as she passed them on leaving the River. She could carry 1,603 people, though her Bay licence was for 1,524. She was also notable for the amount of smoke that could gush from her single funnel. Arriving from England via Surabaya and Thursday Island on 4 August, Captain Edward Baird had experienced very little rough weather. She was able to relieve the *Koopa* when she was undergoing her annual overhaul. Unfortunately, Captain Baird killed himself on 9 August and was replaced by Captain Johnston, who was in turn replaced aboard the *Koopa* by Captain J. S. Gibson who had command of the *Beaver* from 1912 until she was paid off in 1948. Meanwhile, the company issued more shares.

Redcliffe jetty seemed always to be a problem, with complaints from a variety of sources, including the local shopkeepers who wanted a proper cargo shed. On Easter Monday 1914 the original jetty was jammed with 1,500 people, who had to be let through the gates in groups of 80. The decking had dangerous holes in 1919 and the tug company complained that the new berth was silting up in 1925. Captain Johnston was unable to berth the *Doomba* owing to an unusually low tide, and so bypassed Redcliffe on 22 March 1924. He was quite unimpressed when the *Doomba* grounded twice at Redcliffe jetty in January 1926, and as a result the tug company refused to pay the increased berthing fees until the berth was made safe. He commented on the ship's good behaviour when she was dashed twice against Redcliffe jetty without significant damage in heavy seas on 16 May 1926.

A few not untypical excursions to Redcliffe aboard the *Koopa* would be the Cribb & Foote employees picnic in 1914 and the State Schools Excursion from the West Moreton district the same year, the Apollo Club male choir in 1917, the Coachbuilders' Federation picnic in 1920, the Ithaca Town Council employees picnic in 1924, the Railway Stores picnic in 1926 and the Christian Endeavour in 1932. These would all usually include sporting events at Suttons Beach. Twice in 1934 the *Koopa* was hired for the Radio Station 4BH picnic, with Uncle Archie leading the community singing.

Elegant and ladylike, *Koopa* shows off her fine lines at Redcliffe jetty in the late 1930s. (Queensland Maritime Museum collection)

The 'pretty little resort' of Redcliffe was seen to be somewhat somnolent during the winter, but as summer came, so did the trippers on the *Koopa* for 'a glorious trip on the finest bay in Australia; everybody, barring the victims of mal-de-mer, enjoying the sun, the sand, the clear water, and the bracing breeze'.

The company was proud to have carried a total of 80,000 passengers during 1923. The Christmases of 1924 and 1925 were perhaps the height of the tug company's excursion operations, when on one day the *Doomba* and *Koopa* made two Bay trips and the *Beaver*, *Otter* and *Greyhound* one each. With the return fare to Bribie at 4/6 with children half price, over £800 was taken, and over 5,000 people made the trip. New Year 1927 was celebrated with full loads aboard the *Koopa* and *Doomba*, and the two Sandgate to Woody Point ferries taking as many and as often as they could. Easter would also see an influx of visitors, with a special 6.45pm sailing from Brisbane on the Thursday night to bring the business people. A New Year crowd would fill the steamer, and in 1934 huge numbers of people were at Redcliffe, with 942 cars parked wherever they could.

The government had sold perpetual leases to property close to the Bribie jetty in 1919, subject to appropriate development, and in 1926, for instance, 50 new houses were built. But at the census in 1933, there were just 170 permanent residents in 72 dwellings. Redcliffe, by contrast, as it straggled along the Bay shores, had a population of 2,008. Facilities at the 'cosy little settlement' of Bongaree might be overwhelmed with excursionists. With the completion of the tug company's road to the ocean beach in 1923, a truck was converted to a bus and passengers could buy a combined boat and bus ticket to take them over and back. Soon there were proper buses, with crossbench seats, just like some of the Brisbane trams.

Bribie Island was a kind of untamed paradise. Mud crabs were plentiful. Also, with a bit of ingenuity you could find groper in the Pumicestone Passage. One of these weighed in at 500 pounds when it was caught in 1929. Campers and holiday makers would be on the lookout for Ned Bishop's boat, which would have food, fruit and vegetables for sale at the jetty. Until she was burned in January 1922, Maloney's motor launch *Calibri* would meet the *Koopa* at Bribie, coming from Caloundra. The 25 mile passage would be done in three hours for a variable fare of around 3/6, depending on passenger numbers. In September 1926 the service was revived by Evan Clarke's *Dorrijean*, capable of taking 40 passengers, for a return fare of 5/- twice a week. This might be, it was suggested, the ‘gateway to the north coast’.

Lantern slide shown in Redcliffe’s movie theatre in *Koopa*’s early years encouraging viewers to visit Bribie Island. (Queensland Maritime Museum collection)

Twelve-year-old Valera Wilson from Miva in the Mary Valley, was holidaying at Redcliffe in March 1928 and was tremendously excited about going to Bribie Island on the *Koopa*. As it rained hard, they had to have their sandwiches for lunch on board, but they could watch the successes of the fishermen on the pier. Visiting the engine room she was told ‘they use five tons of coal on the round trip from Brisbane to Bribie Island'. Sailing at 2.30pm she sat on the stern 'watching sharks and porpoises swimming round the boat'. Rain or not, she had a wonderful day.

Captain Johnston left for a holiday in England on 25 March 1924, and his departure on the *Euripedes* was saluted by the *Koopa* as she came up to the mouth of the River under the command of Captain N. A. Davies. As the evening light fell, the liner was followed out by the *Clan Mactavish* and the *Theseus*.

There was trouble on board on 3 October 1925 when drunken youths annoyed the other passengers. Despite a warning, Henry Wilson had to be confined on board when the ship arrived at Redcliffe and handed over to the Water Police on return to Petrie Bight. When his friend John Hurley attempted to free him from their custody, he was also run in, with assistance from the ship's officers, and both were fined £2 or prison terms in default.

The 'fierce competition of the car' and declining economic conditions during the latter part of the 1920s slowly whittled away the business. The *Doomba* was withdrawn from regular running in 1928, though she was not finally laid up until 1936. The company was trying in vain to sell her in 1937 and 1938. The *Greyhound* was sold for work in Geelong in 1926. 34 calls by the *Koopa* in May 1928 had brought only 966 passengers to Redcliffe, and there was a serious possibility that the whole service might be withdrawn. Operation remained financially marginal through the 1930s. On 4 October 1935 the Hornibrook Highway was opened; a long wooden toll bridge linking the Redcliffe peninsula with Sandgate across the shallow waters of Bramble Bay. It was said to be the longest viaduct in Australia and it allowed a huge increase in vehicle numbers. Cars paid 1/- and pushbikes 3d. Importantly, a coordinated rail and bus service was introduced with the new bridge, with a return fare from Brisbane to Margate of 3/3 on weekdays and 2/9 on weekends and holidays. It was cheaper than the ships, and faster. This vital road link, along with improvements to the Old Brisbane Road via Petrie, marked the end of the real need for a Redcliffe ferry service. The Hornibrook

Highway had two humps so that small craft could pass underneath into Hays Inlet and the Pine River. The Petrie road, though, remained very rough and flood-prone. The *Olivine* had gone to the Northern Territory in 1929 and the rails and trolleys from Woody Point jetty were sold to Evans Deakin. Sometimes the *Koopa* would not call at Redcliffe on her way back from Bribie. Indeed, a Bribie excursion could be so popular that at Easter 1937 the *Beaver* was required to take the overflow. At 12.5 knots, she was a lot slower than the *Koopa*.

Noted for her speed, *Koopa* overtakes the Hayles launch *Mirimar* during 1937. (photo by Heather Jones, C & D Jones collection)

Wild weather could sometimes be experienced, with the notorious Brisbane summer storms. Captain Johnston was an expert, bringing the ship safely alongside at Redcliffe despite a boisterous south-easter. On 9 February 1915 the weather forecasters advised that the *Olivine* should leave Woody Point and take shelter in the nearest river. The *Koopa* maintained her usual run, but had to come as close as 150 yards from Redcliffe Jetty before it could be seen. The heavy manila mooring lines were repeatedly carried away and seas broke over the upper deck before she sailed for home. With coastal shipping held in port, the *Koopa* was described as having 'an exciting time'. On 30 December 1920 the mainmast was struck by lightning during a thunderstorm. She was not affected by a waterspout on the Bay on 24 May 1921, though everyone had a good view. On 8 January 1928 there was what was described as a sudden cyclonic storm, which hit the *Koopa* just as she was backing out from Redcliffe jetty. The return voyage to Brisbane was most uncomfortable, with violent rain squalls soaking everyone on the upper deck, despite canvas weather curtains, and water also getting into the main saloon areas. In a gale that blew for 24 hours, Captain Johnston tried to come in to Redliffe, where waves were breaking over the end of the jetty, at 4pm on 28 December 1933, but gave up and continued direct to Brisbane, as seas broke some of the port side windows. On 24 July 1938, on the other hand, she ran into dense fog on the way downstream on her evening showboat cruise and had to unload 400 disgruntled passengers at Brett's Wharf to make their own way home by tram and taxi. You could barely see half the length of the ship. As the fog thinned upstream, she waited and made her way back to the city. Later, on 16 January 1949, she had to anchor in mid channel off Luggage Point because the fierce dark stormy conditions made it impossible to pick up the river beacons.

On another occasion, when a strong fresh had the River running at six knots, a number of large ships chose to anchor by the Pile Light. On 28 January 1927 the *Koopa* acted as tender to the Orient Line's *Orsova*, bringing her passengers up to the city and taking others down. She did a similar service for the passengers of the *Orvieto*, which berthed at Borthwick's Wharf in June 1930. Flood waters could bring down masses of hyacinth, at which times she had to be eased out of the wharf in the River so the weed would not foul her screws. On 2 February 1931, when flood waters reached as high as 12'10" at the Port Office and all shipping was ordered to clear the River, the *Koopa* was kept in steam all day to help in any emergency.

On 17 May 1929 the *Koopa* was hired for a cruise around the southern part of the Bay for delegates to the Chambers of Commerce Congress. The Brisbane people ribbed those from Sydney about the relative size of their harbours. Miss Emma Stewart's Jazz Orchestra was cheered when it played the 'Brisbane national anthem', Yes, We Have No Bananas, and Webster & Co's catering was voted fit for a Cunard liner.

Koopa shows off her newly painted dark green hull and black funnels received during a makeover in 1936. (photo by Heather Jones, C & D Jones collection)

Fares in 1934 were 4/6 return and 3/- single, with 1/- children single or return. Passengers might be warned to be on board in a timely manner so the ship could be past Fort Lytton before 10.30am gunnery practice. The *Koopa* was still very popular, and in 1935 she was refitted, when some of the main deck windows were partly plated up and the forward part of the promenade deck enclosed. When she emerged in August 1936 she sported a smart new colour scheme. Her hull had been repainted dark green and her funnels black with a red band, the original colours of the

Brisbane Tug Company. This did not last, as the funnels were soon changed to yellow with a red band and the hull to its original grey after eighteen months.

In 1934 new competition arose in the excursion trade with the advent of the *Mirimar*. The enterprising Hayles Company, proprietors of motor launches at Townsville and Cairns, expanded their business to Brisbane with this larger vessel. She was licensed for 240 passengers on the Bay and ran excursions complementary to those of the *Koopa*, to Amity Point on Stradbroke Island, and other points in the southern part of the Bay. Amity Point – you could buy a block of land there that might be at the bottom of the sea from erosion by next year. In 1936 she was joined by a small sister, the *Mirabel* for 110 passengers. Both boats were good for a little over ten knots. Among several rivals was the *Lookout*, built in 1939.

Koopa being met at Redcliffe by a relaxed crowd in 1952. The authors' parents are in the lower left of this picture. (photo by Ken Rogers, John Oxley Library, State Library of Queensland neg.37296)

For young people, and families who did not own a car, a Bay trip was a cheap and rewarding excursion, in the cool breezes away from the city heat. If there were a sale at one of the big Valley stores, you might even squeeze in a visit there before the ship sailed. There were also some famous moonlight cruises, often with one of the theatre bands aboard. In January 1930, for instance, one was hosted by the GPS Old Boys' Rowing Club, and in other years during the 1930s the Garage and Service Stations' Association had a Hawaiian orchestra for the dancing. There were many special day trips. A voyage on the *Koopa* was a very satisfactory finale to the Queensland Butter and Cheese Factory Managers' Association annual conference in June 1928. On 12 November 1934 the annual Lockyer Bay Trip used special express trains to bring people to the *Koopa.* The Toowoomba departure was at 4am and Marburg at 6am. Country people could escape for a day from the 'hot muggy inland' to the breezy decks of the steamer to take in the ozone. The Central Methodist Mission sponsored an annual cruise between 1932 and 1936. E. B. Maher MLA, the leader of the Country Party in Parliament, booked a regular annual excursion in the period between 1936 and 1941, though with the proviso that any overflow of passengers would have to go to Sandgate by train. 290 boys from the Young Australia League were aboard in August 1937. Interstate RSL visitors took a cruise in March 1938. Maybe on a regular Bribie run there would be a tune on the piano-accordion by Porky Jones on the return trip, and a general sing-along. A moonlight cruise was sponsored by radio station 4BC, on 23 October 1934, but for 4BH on Christmas Eve 1937, when dance music was to be broadcast, the radio relay equipment failed to perform, much to the chagrin of all concerned, and especially the operator on the ship, who proceeded to throw all of the useless hardware into the river.

The *Koopa* was in collision with the steamer *Wandana* in the bend of the River at New Farm on 28 March 1940, with minor damage. There were also rescues. On 24 March 1940, Colin Bonner and three friends clung to their overturned skiff off Scarborough for over three hours before being rescued by the *Koopa*. On 23

February the following year, Gordon Jackson and two friends were in a similar predicament for two hours before their cooees were heard and the ship stopped to rescue them. In both cases it had been decided that attempting to swim to shore was too dangerous.

For the Town of Redcliffe, although Captain Johnston had complained about the decay of the fender piles in 1936, there was a new art deco arch with dressing sheds built at the end of the jetty in 1938, and the shelter shed converted into an amusement hall. With a real sense of progress, Redcliffe received its first piped town water in 1941 and its own Luna Park in 1944. At the age of 30 the *Koopa* seemed to be a fixture on the Bay. But an era of excursions had to be put on hold.

Koopa arrives at Redcliffe during a holiday afternoon in January 1951. (photo by Heather Jones, C & D Jones collection ©)

During the Second World War the Australian coast was scoured of its beautiful excursion vessels to fulfil minor naval roles. The *Doomba* was requisitioned and purchased by the Royal Australian Navy early, in view of her naval origin, and commissioned as a minesweeper on 25 September 1939. The *Koopa* was taken on 10 August 1942, as the war in the Pacific came closer. She was commissioned into the Royal Australian Navy in Brisbane on 14 September 1942 with 40 crew commanded by Lieutenant Commander G. W. T. Armstrong. Brisbane was full of the army and there was little thought for excursions. Navigation was restricted by the boom at Lytton. Also, Bribie had become a military area, with the building of forts with heavy guns to command the shipping channels.

HMAS *Koopa* bristles with anti-aircraft guns after being taken over by the Navy in 1942. (Australian War Memorial image.PO1993-004-1)

At Toorbul Point Combined Training School, after the *Koopa* arrived on 22 September, she had to be sent back to Brisbane to have a ramp fitted for launching the army's Mark III folding boats, of which 24 were carried. One of the locals, Terry Green, used to come by in his boat. 'Leave the old girl alone', he would shout. From 21 October 1942 she was involved in training US marines in combined operations landings, using the beaches on Moreton Island. The folding boats were now replaced with US army landing craft. The last Australian unit completed training at Toorbul in March 1943.

She then served as a mother ship for Fairmile B motor launches, first at their Toorbul Point base, and then in the New Guinea area, sailing from Townsville to Port Moresby as part of convoy TN172 in October 1943. The Fairmiles were worked hard on patrol, escort and inshore offensive tasks. Being a coal-burning ship in a region where that commodity was in short supply, the *Koopa* was frequently towed and kept with full bunkers in case it was necessary for her to escape somewhere hurriedly under her own power. She had two 20mm anti-aircraft guns as well as machine guns, full wireless gear, and an extra coal storage bunker on the open promenade deck between the funnels. A crew of 45 included men to operate lathes and other equipment. At Milne Bay, the furthest place where coal was available, she coaled from the lighter *Rona*. It was a hot and dirty business, leaving the entire crew black and grimy with only their eyes showing. In the Madang area she was often in company with the *Bingera*, *Laurabada* and *Ping Wo*.

In the Wewak area she evacuated soldiers struck with typhus and on one occasion had the embarrassing experience of having the wire of an experimental anti-aircraft rocket wrap itself around one of the screws. For Operation Hunter out of Mios Woendi atoll, near Biak in Dutch New Guinea in August 1944, she was towed by the tug *Wato*, herself a coal burner and the oldest ship in the navy, and was the base for eight motor launches undertaking anti-submarine sweeps. They called her 'the Ark'. Here the Australians were part of Task Group 70.1, a small part of the mighty US Seventh Fleet preparing for the invasion of the Philippines, along with 100 American PT boats operating against Japanese supply lines. It was one of the most exposed forward positions occupied by the Allies, and Japanese bombers came over most nights, to be engaged by the night fighters. In Mios she was partly careened to get rid of barnacles. Brisbane men, serving in the islands, saw and remembered her with great affection, though her facilities were less lavish than those of American support ships such as the *Mobjack*, *Portunus* and *Hilo*. She was under the command of a succession of officers, including Lieutenant Norman Wallis RANVR, a keen yachtsman and chess fanatic. Always a good raconteur, especially in regard to his schooner *Wanderer*, now serving with the RAN, he was promoted to command of the corvette *Gympie* in September 1944.

HMAS *Koopa* at Alexishafen, Madang, with a group of Fairmile motor launches. (Australian War Memorial image.073975-2)

She left Madang in tow of the tug *Tancred* on 27 January 1945, to arrive in Brisbane on 11 February. On the way, the *Koopa* had to take shelter from a cyclone in the lee of the Palm Islands near Ingham, which at this time had its heaviest rainfall ever. Although she pitched and tossed violently, with all the crew on the upper deck in life jackets, Lieutenant John Stephens in command praised her as 'tough and seaworthy'. She was briefly transferred to the

RN on 26 July as a floating power station, but was back in the RAN on 24 September.

Koopa running trials on 8 January 1947 before resuming commercial service after the war. (Queensland Maritime Museum collection)

In November 1946 a refit began to convert her for commercial service and she was returned to her owners on 10 January 1947. She re-entered the Bribie service on 4 February. That she came back at all in this period when other famous ships such as Melbourne's *Weeroona* did not, was something very special for the people of Brisbane. The Navy even gave her new screws and on trials she logged 15.6 knots. Captain Johnston had died in June 1946, so her new master was Captain J. A. R. Davis.

But the post-war days were not good for her, especially after the 1950 lifting of petrol rationing, and with the competition of more Hayles launches. The Scarborough to Bribie route also had a small ferry, though she was burned in April 1947 and had to be replaced. The *Beaver* had been sold in 1940, so with the proceeds of this and the sale of the *Doomba* the company had been able to repay capital, but whenever the *Koopa* was laid up for repair or overhaul a Hayles launch had to be hired to take over the Bribie run. Passenger numbers fell, though there were still special events, such as a talent quest on board in 1950, recorded by Brisbane's newest radio station, 4KQ.

Koopa steams down Hamilton Reach in August 1950 on her first voyage with a white hull. Cloudland ballroom and the interstate passenger liner *Manunda* are in the background. (Queensland Maritime Museum collection)

Another was an excursion for 300 children from orphanages and State Homes on 19 January 1950, sponsored by the social club of the coastal steamer *Elsanna* while she was in dock. There were glamourous occasions too. Church of England young people arranged a moonlight dance cruise on 27 November 1952 to mark the end of their university exams. The Red Cross held a "semi-ball" on the *Koopa* in the previous May.

Severe weather saw the *Koopa* unable to call at Redcliffe on three successive days in January 1951. Finally, with the government refusing to help with a subsidy, she was advertised for sale in May 1951. After a deal of public disquiet, she and the tug company's properties on Bribie were eventually bought by a local syndicate called the Moreton Bay Development Coy. Ltd.

As part of the Moreton Bay Development Company's support for Bribie Island, *Koopa* rests at Bongaree jetty. (Queensland Maritime Museum collection)

Her new master, Captain John Marion, did not start well, as on 16 February 1952, her first day under the new management, the *Koopa* hit the Redcliffe jetty with such an impact as to seriously damage the structure. Concrete piles were broken, and heavy planks were flung in the air while people ran for safety. The jetty had already shown signs of deterioration in 1946. Marion claimed to have misjudged the vessel's speed. Compared with the jetty, the ship demonstrated her sturdy construction. Marion was replaced by the experienced Captain T. J. Robertson, who had retired in 1949 after

21 years as Brisbane Harbour Master. Meanwhile there were as many as 150 applications from young women to staff the dining room and milk bar.

Rising costs of the early 1950s are reflected in the *Koopa*'s timetable and fare structure. (Queensland Maritime Museum collection)

Thursday, Saturday, Sunday and holidays she left for Redcliffe and Bribie at 9am, and at 7.45pm Sunday and 8pm Friday there were dance cruises, with Frank Jeffers and the Koopa Orchestra, and comperes Norman Llewellyn and Johnny James of radio station 4BH. There was even an occasional mannequin parade.

It did not last. The company was poorly capitalised in an environment of high inflation and the government still would not help. She ran her last trip on 4 May 1953, farewelled at Bribie like the departure of an ocean liner, with streamers from people on the jetty. The company went into voluntary liquidation on the 25th. At the advanced age of 42, the *Koopa* was laid up at Kangaroo Point, eventually being sold to Noel Malmstedt who intended to install two diesel engines to convert her for cargo work in the Bay.

Veteran Captain T. J. Robertson brings *Koopa* alongside Redcliffe jetty in January 1953. (photos by Mervyn Jones, C & D Jones collection ©)

Rust stained and in her final summer, *Koopa* pulls away from Redcliffe jetty on 15 January 1953. (photo by Mervyn Jones, C & D Jones collection ©)

Fortunately for the image of the ship, the scheme ran into difficulties, and the *Koopa* then lay against a disused wharf at South Brisbane. Sometimes people came just to stand on her deck, their eyes misty with nostalgia. The wharf at Circular Quay was leased for a car park. Eventually she was taken away to be scrapped in 1961 at Boggy Creek, Myrtletown. Among the relics, her Oregon pine mainmast became a flagpole for St Paul's School, Bald Hills, drawn out of the ship by a TAA Hiller helicopter. Her whistle went to Redbank Meatworks. Her Redcliffe and Bribie run was inherited by the *Mirimar*, while the *Mirana* ran the regular Amity Point and Dunwich service. Bribie had a very basic car ferry service from Toorbul Point provided by an old army ALC20 landing barge with a capacity of 25 tons in sheltered waters. Then with the bridge at Toorbul Point, opened in 1963, and the sad decay of the Redcliffe jetty, ships no longer called at either place.

Because of the unsafe condition of the Redcliffe jetty, Hayles refused to serve it after 1961. The last Hayles passenger ferry to Stradbroke Island ran in 1977, squeezed out by vehicular ferries to the island. Services to Bishop Island finished in 1980. There are now no regular Bay excursions at all, except for the Tangalooma ferry, though the new Redcliffe jetty built with a breakwater in 1999 encouraged a Bay cruise boat, *Eye Spy*, to operate from it. It is a lot harder to find wildflowers too. They are all covered by houses. The River itself is different. Fisherman Islands and Bishop Island alike are no more, swallowed up in vast new port developments. The big ships no longer come upstream. The wharves are demolished. If you want to go anywhere, you take your own boat. It is not necessarily a change for the better.

But there is another *Koopa.* A new cross-river ferry took the name in honour of the old ship, long in love, when she entered service in 1986. There is a *Doomba* too, and an *Otter*. Though nothing like their namesakes, they keep the memory alive.

Koopa's name still lives on as a cross-river ferry (photo by Colin Jones)

Conversion Tables

Throughout SS *Koopa*'s life weights and measures followed the Imperial system and currency was in pounds, shillings and pence.

Linear measurement:

1 inch (1")	=	2.54 centimetres
1 foot (1')	=	0.3048 metre
1 yard	=	0.9144 metre
1 statute mile	=	1.6093 kilometres
1 nautical mile	=	1.8519 kilometres

Weight:

1 pound	=	0.4536 kilograms
1 ton	=	1016.05 kilograms

Engine power:

Indicated horsepower (ihp) measures input into the engine using an indicator card in an attachment to the engine to compute effective pressure.

1 horsepower (hp)	=	0.746 kilowatts

Boiler pressure:

1 pound per square inch (psi)	=	6.895 kiloPascals

Currency:

1 pound (20 shillings in 1 pound, £1) = 2 dollars ($2)
1 shilling (12 pence in 1 shilling, 1/-) = 10 cents (10c)
1 penny (1d) = 1 cent (1c)

Direct financial comparisons are misleading due to the effect of inflation over many years. As an example, a return fare to Redcliffe aboard the *Koopa* was two shillings and sixpence (2/6) when she commenced service in 1911, but had trebled to seven shillings and sixpence (7/6) when she was paid off over forty years later.

Bibliography

Abrahams, Audrey, *Brothers of Bribie Heritage*, privately published, Brisbane, 1999

Bastock, John, *Australia's Ships of War*, Angus & Robertson, Sydney, 1975

Bryant, John, 'The War Cruise of the Koopa', in *Canberra Times*, 31 December 1995

Donald, Ron, *The Queen of Moreton Bay*, Victory Press, Bribie, 2008

Donald, Ron, *The Yanks called it "Terrible Point"*, Victory Press, Bribie, 2010

Evans, Peter & Thomson, Richard, *Fairmile Ships of the Royal Australian Navy*, Vol 2, Australian Military History for the Fairmile Association, Sydney, 2005

Gee, Patricia, *Jetty Memories*, Boolarong, Brisbane, 1999

Gee, Patricia & Smith, Michelle, eds, *Redcliffe Remembers*, Redcliffe City Council, Redcliffe, 2004

Gee, Patricia, *Boats on the Bay*, Moreton Bay Regional Council, Caboolture, 2011

Gregory, Helen, *The Brisbane River Story*, Australian Marine Conservation Society, Brisbane, 1996

Groom, Neil, *The Sunday Mail Nostalgia Book*, Queensland Newspapers, Brisbane, 1986

Harte, Bernard, *When Radio was the Cat's Whiskers*, Rosenberg, Sydney, 2002, reprint of 1993 original

Jones, Michael, *Redcliffe*, Allen & Unwin, Sydney, 1988

Ludlow, Peter, *Moreton Bay People*, privately published, Brisbane, 2000

Ludlow, Peter, *Moreton Bay Letters*, privately published, Brisbane, 2003

Nesdale, Iris, *Small Ships at War*, privately published, Adelaide, 1993

Nolan, Carolyn & Longhurst, Robert, *Brisbane's Moreton Bay*, State Library of Queensland, Brisbane, 1996

Pfennigwerth, Ian, *The Royal Australian Navy and MacArthur*, Rosenberg, Dural NSW, 2009
Rhys, Lloyd, *My Ship is So Small*, Georgian House, Melbourne, 1946
Slaughter, Leslie, *Redcliffe's 150 Years*, Redcliffe Town Council, Brisbane, 1959
Solley, K. E., *Brisbane Tug & Steamship Co Ltd*, privately published typescript, Brisbane, 1956, revised edition, Sydney, 1975
The Brisbane Courier, various issues
The Courier Mail, various issues
The Queenslander, various issues
The Sunday Mail, various issues
Tompkins, Robert, *Compendium of Australasian Merchant Ships 1831 – 2008*, Nautical Association of Australia, Melbourne, 2008
Torrance, William, *Steamers on the River*, privately published, Brisbane, 1986
T. R. C., 'A Trip to Brisbane: Redcliffe', in *Advertiser* (Footscray) 25 March 1916
Tutt, Stan, *Pioneer Days*, Caboolture Historical Society, Nambour, 1974
Welsby, Thomas, *Bribie, the Basket Maker*, Barkers, Brisbane, 1937
Wilson, Valera, 'A Day on the 'Koopa', in *Australasian*, 17 March 1928

Index

About the Authors

Colin and David Jones were born and brought up in Brisbane where they gained a life-long interest in shipping, observing vessels on the river and going on family excursions on Moreton Bay. Both have retired after careers in the Public Service, Colin with the Commonwealth Government in Melbourne, and David with the Queensland Audit Office. They continue to pursue their interest in maritime history by research, writing and public speaking. Colin is actively involved in the World Ship Society, Victoria, and David volunteers at the Queensland Maritime Museum. With their wives, Robyn and Heather respectively, they gain further enjoyment from their families and grandchildren, and in travel.

Maritime books published by Colin and David are:

Patrol Boat Story, by Colin and David Jones (1972)
The Whalers of Tangalooma, by David Jones (1980)
Ferries on the Yarra, by Colin Jones (1981)
Australian Colonial Navies, by Colin Jones (1986)
Wings and the Navy, by Colin Jones (1997)
Steamboat Memories, by Colin Jones (2001)
US Subs Down Under, by David Jones and Peter Nunan (2005) re-published as *Subs Down Under* (2011)
Wings on the River, by David Jones (2007)
Master Mariner, by David Jones and Peter Nunan (2009)
Royalty & the River, by David Jones (2012)
More Than a Haircut and Shave, by David Jones & Peter Nunan (2013)